First Facts®

Animal Rulers

KINGS OF THE MOUNTAINS

by Rebecca Rissman

Consultant:
Jackie Gai, DVM
Wildlife Veterinarian

CAPSTONE PRESS
a capstone imprint

First Facts are published by Capstone Press,
1710 Roe Crest Drive, North Mankato, Minnesota 56003
www.mycapstone.com

Library of Congress Cataloging-in-Publication Data
Library of Congress Cataloging-in-Publication Data is available on the Library
of Congress website.

ISBN: 978-1-5157-8067-0 (library binding) — 978-1-5157-8073-1 (paperback) —
978-1-5157-8079-3 (eBook PDF)

Summary: Learn about the animal rulers in the mountains.

Editorial Credits
Adrian Vigliano, editor; Kayla Rossow, designer; Kelly Garvin, media researcher;
Kathy McColley, production specialist

Photo Credits
Shutterstock: Ammit Jack, 13, Baranov E, 11, Dennis Jacobsen, 19, Dennis W.
Donohue, 15, dptro, cover (top left), FCG, 17, leeloona, cover (top middle), Matt
Jeppson, 21, Michal Ninger, cover (top right), My Good Images, 5, Petr Kopka,
cover (middle), Photo West 7, robert cicchetti, cover (bottom), Scott E. Read, 9

Artistic Elements
Shutterstock: Alexander Yu. Zotov, Alexvectors, blambca, By, Gallinago_media,
Galyna Andrushko, iconizer, Les Perysty, nanovector, Nikolay Se, Petrovic Igor,
oorka, robert cicchetti, steffiheufelder, Yoko Design

Printed and bound in China.
004727

Table of Contents

On Top of the Mountain

High in the mountains, a few animals rule. Giant wings swoop. Sharp fangs bite. Deadly claws swipe.

Mountain rulers have **adapted** to control other mountain animals. They have few **predators**. They travel large distances. Some are skilled hunters.

adapt—to change to fit into a new or different environment
predator—an animal that hunts other animals for food

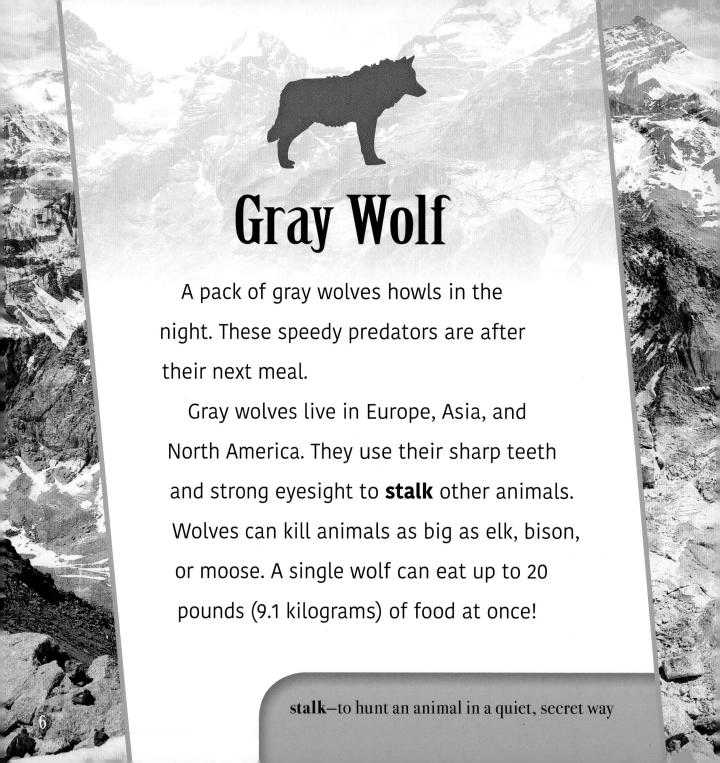

Gray Wolf

A pack of gray wolves howls in the night. These speedy predators are after their next meal.

Gray wolves live in Europe, Asia, and North America. They use their sharp teeth and strong eyesight to **stalk** other animals. Wolves can kill animals as big as elk, bison, or moose. A single wolf can eat up to 20 pounds (9.1 kilograms) of food at once!

stalk—to hunt an animal in a quiet, secret way

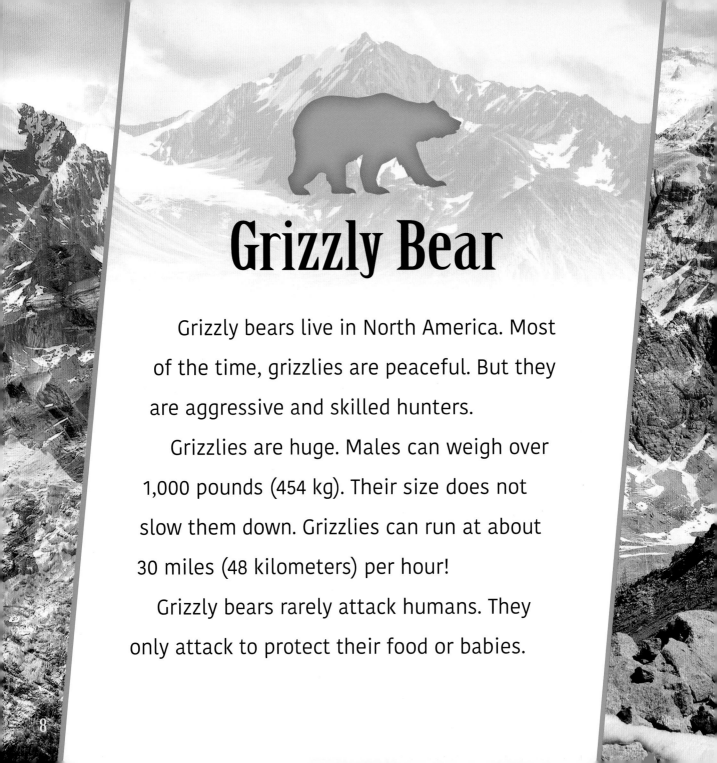

Grizzly Bear

Grizzly bears live in North America. Most of the time, grizzlies are peaceful. But they are aggressive and skilled hunters.

Grizzlies are huge. Males can weigh over 1,000 pounds (454 kg). Their size does not slow them down. Grizzlies can run at about 30 miles (48 kilometers) per hour!

Grizzly bears rarely attack humans. They only attack to protect their food or babies.

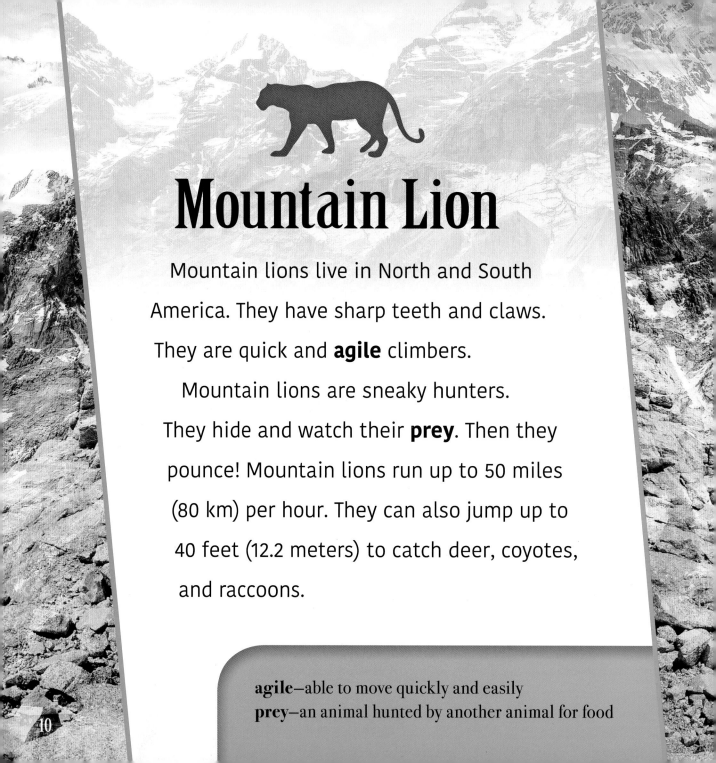

Mountain Lion

Mountain lions live in North and South America. They have sharp teeth and claws. They are quick and **agile** climbers.

Mountain lions are sneaky hunters. They hide and watch their **prey**. Then they pounce! Mountain lions run up to 50 miles (80 km) per hour. They can also jump up to 40 feet (12.2 meters) to catch deer, coyotes, and raccoons.

agile—able to move quickly and easily
prey—an animal hunted by another animal for food

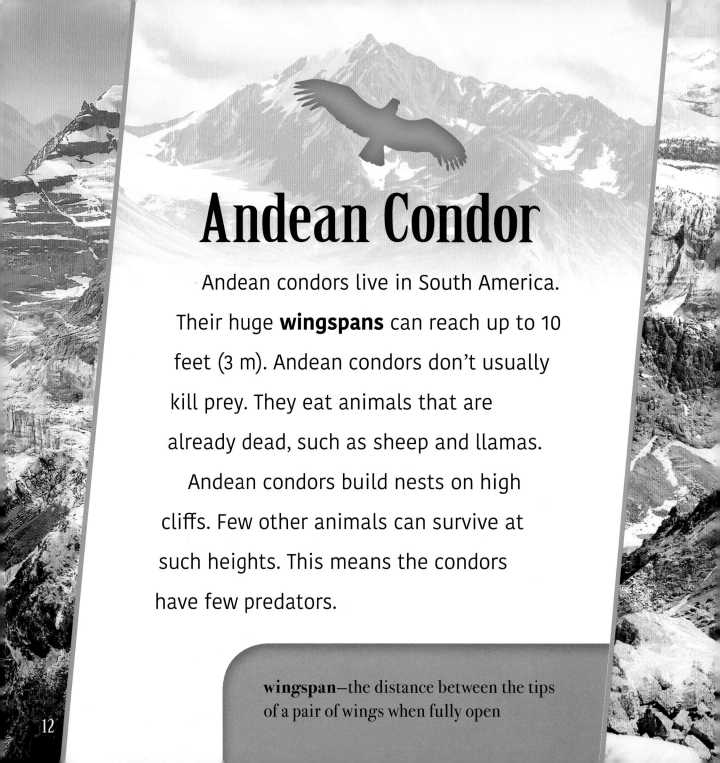

Andean Condor

Andean condors live in South America. Their huge **wingspans** can reach up to 10 feet (3 m). Andean condors don't usually kill prey. They eat animals that are already dead, such as sheep and llamas. Andean condors build nests on high cliffs. Few other animals can survive at such heights. This means the condors have few predators.

wingspan—the distance between the tips of a pair of wings when fully open

Fact! Human activity threatens some mountain rulers. Andean condors are threatened by human hunting.

13

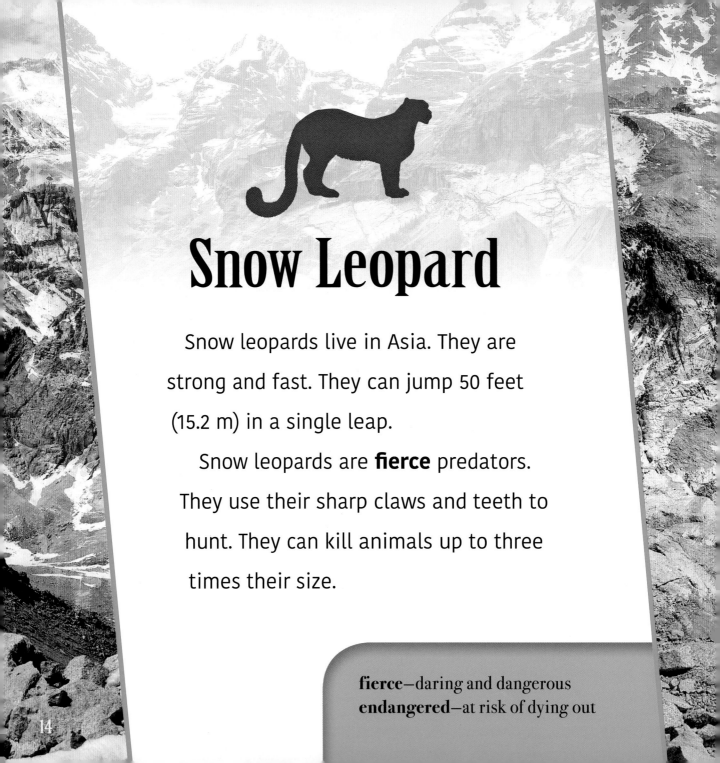

Snow Leopard

Snow leopards live in Asia. They are strong and fast. They can jump 50 feet (15.2 m) in a single leap.

Snow leopards are **fierce** predators. They use their sharp claws and teeth to hunt. They can kill animals up to three times their size.

fierce—daring and dangerous
endangered—at risk of dying out

Fact! Snow leopards are **endangered**. Sometimes, humans hunt snow leopards for their thick, beautiful fur.

15

Mountain Gorilla

Mountain gorillas live in Africa. They
eat plants and are usually very gentle.
But these gorillas rule the mountains.
Mountain gorillas live in groups.
A large male called a silverback
leads each group. If a silverback feels
threatened, he pounds his chest and
roars. Sometimes, he even attacks!
Silverbacks punch, shove, and bite.

food chain—a series of plants and animals in which
each one in the series eats the one before it

Fact! All living things are part of a **food chain**. Mountain gorillas are at the top of their food chain. This means they have few predators.

Wolverine

Wolverines have sharp claws and deadly teeth. Wolverines usually hunt small animals such as rabbits. Sometimes they hunt prey as large as caribou! Wolverines live in North America, Asia, and Europe.

Wolverines are dedicated hunters. They will travel up to 15 miles (24.1 km) a day for food. They will also dig to eat animals hiding in **burrows**.

burrow—a tunnel or hole in the ground made or used by an animal

Timber Rattlesnake

Rattle, rattle! A timber rattlesnake makes a warning sound. It may be about to attack! Timber rattlesnakes live in North America. They have a deadly bite. Their sharp fangs contain **venom** strong enough to kill large animals. However, timber rattlesnakes usually eat small birds and mammals.

venom—a poisonous liquid made by an animal to kill its prey

Fact! Timber rattlesnakes only attack humans if they feel threatened.

Glossary

adapt (uh-DAPT)—to change to fit into a new or different environment

agile (AJ-ahyl)—able to move quickly and easily

burrow (BUHR-oh)—a tunnel or hole in the ground made or used by an animal

endangered (in-DAYN-juhrd)—at risk of dying out

fierce (FEERSS)—daring and dangerous

food chain (FOOD CHAYN)—a series of plants and animals in which each one in the series eats the one before it

predator (PRED-uh-tur)—an animal that hunts other animals for food

prey (PRAY)—an animal hunted by another animal for food

stalk (STAWK)—to hunt an animal in a quiet, secret way

venom (VEN-uhm)—a poisonous liquid made by an animal to kill its prey

wingspan (WING-span)—the distance between the tips of a pair of wings when fully open

Read More

Hirsch, Rebecca Eileen. *Mountain Gorillas: Powerful Forest Mammals*. Comparing Animal Traits. Minneapolis: Lerner Publications Company, 2015.

Kolpin, Molly. *Grizzly Bears*. Bears. North Mankato, Minn.: Capstone Press, 2012.

Polinsky, Paige V. *Wolverine: Powerful Predator*. Animal Superstars. Minneapolis: Abdo Publishing, 2016.

Internet Sites

Use Facthound to find Internet sites related to this book.

Visit *www.facthound.com*

Just type in 9781515780670 and go!

Check out projects, games and lots more at
www.capstonekids.com

Critical Thinking Questions

1. Describe the way a silverback fights. Why does this behavior make it a fierce animal?

2. Explain some qualities that help animals rule their habitat. Think about animals that live in extreme habitats, or animals that are very good hunters.

3. What do you think would happen if any one of these large predators were to die out? How would their disappearance affect the habitat?

Index